De Grazia's

Borderlands Sketches

*Native People of Arizona and Sonora
as Drawn by Ted De Grazia*

*Marion DeGrazia
1998*

with drawings collected by Marion De Grazia
and a memoir by Elizabeth Shaw

The Southwest Center
Tucson

Published by

The Southwest Center
The University of Arizona
1052 North Highland Avenue
Tucson, Arizona 85721

Copyright © 1997 The Arizona Board of Regents
All rights reserved

Illustrations © 1997 De Grazia Art and Cultural Foundation
No images herein may be reproduced without the permission
of the De Grazia Gallery, Tucson, Arizona.

Manufactured in the United States of America
Printed on recycled paper

Library of Congress Catalog Card Number 97-67257
ISBN 0-9659296-0-4

De Grazia, Painter of Children and Angels

Artist Ted De Grazia was an Arizonan, born in 1909 in the mining town of Morenci and living most of his life in homemade adobe buildings on the outskirts of Tucson, the desert city in which he died in 1982. In drawing, painting, sculpture, ceramics, and desert architecture, De Grazia rarely if ever depicted the more familiar icons of American life: not the city, not modern buildings or highways, not machines or their products, not the people of the comfortable middle class or any of the objects or environments that provide the backdrop for their daily lives.

Was De Grazia's approach exotic? Probably not. Most of the time he used his own hands and energies, stayed at home in southern Arizona, and focused on the borderlands around him. Much of what he saw and depicted was derivative—from

earlier days in Mexico and even earlier in Spain, from the tribal life and customs and spirit of several distinct groups of Native Americans, the fabric of their lives even now displaying language, custom, usage, religion, food, and modes of survival that differ strikingly from what is referred to as "typically American." Was De Grazia's material foreign? Or do its range and variety simply remind us of what it really means to be American?

Today, the stunning diversity of American society is on its way to becoming a myth that attracts many people and repels others. Like most myths it symbolizes some profound truth. From the east to the west coast of the continent, from southern shores to northern forests, the nation evolved from the actions of men and women coming from almost everywhere. The reality of this in our own times is probably nowhere more clearly demonstrated than in the southwest borderlands. California, Arizona, New Mexico, and Texas share borders with Mexico. By way of Mexico we pass to Central America, to South America, and thus to another continent and to many other worlds, some of them mythical in their own right.

As a feature writer for *The Arizona Daily Star*, fifty years ago I went to interview De Grazia, who lived with his family in a compound of adobe squares he had built at the corner of Prince and Campbell, then a rural chunk of desert outside the city limits, now a traffic-light intersection complete with strip mall, apartment buildings and townhouses.

From candlelit room to room we walked, peering at paintings slanted in corners, piled on tables, stacked on rough shelving. The range of De Grazia's preoccupations was observable: cartridge-belted white-clad peons massing for action; urchins of Mexico, fluting, dancing, hawking, or begging their way through dusty streets flanked by square houses; gossamer angels blowing stars out of celestial trumpets. Children and angels alike had wispy black, black hair, topping faces that were puzzling abstractions of trust and poverty. And there was the gaunt, weary face of Christ, tear-marked and tragically imprinted on the veil of Veronica, one of De Grazia's favorite early paintings.

De Grazia was born to an Italian immigrant family. His father was a miner. Arizona was not yet a state. Ted lived the life of a mining camp child for a decade. Work, play, family, and devout

religious faith were keynotes of daily existence. Ted remembered making a clay head of Christ, then sneaking it into his mother's oven, a place so sacrosanct that even this pious artifact was not admissible. He remembered a mail-order folding figure of a life-sized Jesus, set up in the house as a kind of family shrine.

When Ted was eleven, the family decided to return to relatives near Pompeii in Italy and perhaps prepare their son for the church as a vocation. De Grazia was an acolyte for a while. He remembered jumping over the convent wall to chat with the nuns and during High Mass ceasing to work the hand-bellows that provided air for the organ, so the music stopped. Whether such childhood memories were related to the abrupt end of his religious calling, De Grazia did not know, but by 1925, when he turned sixteen, the family returned to Morenci, and Ted was back in public school.

He said he never liked school and thinks he was a poor pupil. Nevertheless, by 1932 Ted De Grazia the hearty, rugged lover of outdoor life and nature, confirmed seeker of gold in dry washes, was enrolled in the University of Arizona. He guessed maybe the Depression made it impossible to do much else. In any case, he spent thirteen years in the

College of Fine Arts, coming out with three degrees: one bachelor of arts in education, another in fine arts, and a master of arts in music. Despite this, De Grazia never acknowledged much influence from the academic world.

In lapses from study, Ted began to travel south. He was always drawn to Mexico. In Mexico City he met both giants of Mexican revolutionary art: Diego Rivera and José Clemente Orozco. Both acknowledged him and predicted he would become one of the outstanding American painters. Rivera said that the gamut of De Grazia's expression ran from "the simple graceful movement of cocks fighting to the understanding of human misery as in the boy playing the violin." He invited De Grazia to spend three months working with him on the murals at the Palacio de Bellas Artes, saying in his

letter that "this may be a contribution to the culture of our united nations." De Grazia was given a one-man show in 1942 at the Palacio, programmed as "a primitive North American painter." The work showed considerable influence from the Mexican Revolution in the sombreroed, rifle-bearing Indian figures, the hovel dwellings, and the earthy realism. Poverty, piety, and the earth were all keystones in De Grazia's work.

Simplicity more and more characterized his approach. His "midnight sketches" became a dash and a swirl. The early stark realism later gave way to swift abstracting line. The poetry of the simple remained paramount in the ever present figures of children and the poor, whether in street scenes, hogans, or even in a Heaven peopled by weightless

seraphims. Indeed, De Grazia painted a kind of dream-texture alike into the fabric of his heavens, into his carnival scenes and Indian ceremonies, into elongated Arabian horses running to the wind—even into historical narrative such as Padre Kino's missionary life among the Indians, a series of paintings that were the heart of a major exhibit in Los Angeles's Southwest Museum in the sixties.

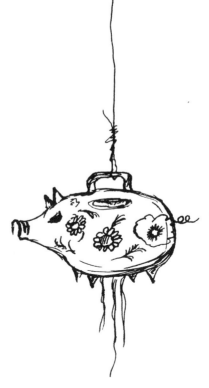

De Grazia insisted that he dreamed his paintings. On the subject of his hero, Padre Kino, he contrived his dream into a legend and published a little book about it called *Padre Nuestro*. From this dream he reported his solitary trek over the Pimería Alta country, visiting Kino's humble dwelling where the ghost of the Padre's Indian housekeeper gave him a

message: that Kino had been waiting for someone to finish his work, to build one final mission in a spot of ultimate beauty—La Iglesia, the rocky summit ridge of the Santa Catalina Mountains on the south side, overlooking the foothills and intermountain plain of Tucson. Right there, beneath the crest, on high ground, is where De Grazia and his Yaqui Indian friends built the little Mission in the Sun. They made it of adobe, on simple lines reminiscent of the old missions. On the evening of feast days its borders are still outlined with luminarias. Inside, the whitewashed walls glow with pastel niños and angels. The nave is open to the mountain crest and the sky and the north light beloved by all artists.

Mysticism was an element in the painter's nature, but as a non-conformist in religion, he maintained to the church the relationship of a loving but canny and critical son. For years he said he turned over all the voluntary offerings from the Mission in the Sun to the priest of a little church in South Tucson. He and the priest always met somewhere in town for the presentation of the money. Repeatedly, Ted suggested that the priest visit the Mission, but somehow it never happened. Finally, De Grazia said, "Father, don't you really want to see where this money has been coming from?" And when there was still neither time nor inclination, Ted made a decision. From then on the money went into a bank account in the name of the Virgin of Guadalupe, patroness of Mexico to whom the Mission is dedicated. Ted added, "When I need to spend some of that money, I just ask her, and since she doesn't say anything, I know it's all right."

The tolerance of saints was not the only thing he took for granted. Broke or affluent, he did not focus consistently on money, and matters of prestige or status seemed unable to affect his choice of friends, his mode of life, or what he was going to do the next minute. Openhanded and generous with impoverished Indian friends, oblivious to many kinds of social distinctions, he himself often heaped up the fuel with which critics tried to burn his reputation. In business deals with such firms as Fuller Fabrics, Hallmark, and the Aaron Ashley Galleries, De Grazia refused to sign contracts, believing they are made to be broken. For years he had working relationships with such enterprises, which reproduced and sold his work.

Royalties, he said, were structured something like this (always verbally)—"The price of a shot of whiskey for a Navajo print, and the price of a good cigar for a Mariachi."

As the decades passed, De Grazia admitted he was becoming more conservative, describing himself as doing many things he had formerly refused to do—going to parties, keeping appointments, going to San Francisco as a guest of honor at a banquet of fine printers, and even going to France. But formal invitations were always a problem. As he saw it, "If I say Monday I'll go Friday, how do I know I'll want to go when Friday comes?"

De Grazia's close friends included many people who were poor and illiterate, who never went to an art show, and had scarcely looked at paintings other than Ted's. But he had also the friendship and respect of Thomas Hart Benton, Olaf Wieghorst, Ross Santee, and other artists and illustrators of his time. Unlike many renowned artists of ages past, De Grazia began to experience fame in the prime of his life. An artist who painted the dictates of his subconscious and his dreams, who had the energy to work long hours every day at his art, he nevertheless dragged his feet just a bit as he mounted the threshold to success.

After all, De Grazia said, what he really wanted was
to be a prospector, to live in the hills, to carry a rifle,
to fight if need be, to cook his food over open fire—
in short, to be like the colorful characters of the old
West. A week before going to Los Angeles for the
big museum show, Ted, with his Yaqui, Papago, and
Anglo cronies, went into Superstition Mountains to
look for the Lost Dutchman Mine, with bedrolls,
horses, guns, and tequila. He liked to show
photographs of the group and their antics that he
seemed to cherish as much as his paintings. This, he
implied, was where he belonged. This was the life
he was intended to lead.

Dante, said Browning, tried to paint an angel, and
Raphael tried to write a sonnet. De Grazia, painter
of children and angels, tried to be a prospector, but
history wasn't about to let it happen.

Elizabeth Shaw

16

The Papagos

Native Name: Tohono O'odham, *1990 Census:* 16,000+

Historically the Papago people's territory (called the Papaguería) stretched from the Río Concepción in Mexico north to the Gila River, west of the Santa Cruz River to the valleys just east of the Colorado River. Today the Papagos are largely seen around the San Xavier and Tohono O'odham reservations west of Tucson and the Gila Bend reservation west of Phoenix. That their reservations were established late, some in the twentieth century, is explained by the Papago people almost always having been allies, first of the Spanish, and then the Americans, against the Apaches.

The Papagos early on were farmers and cattle ranchers and in later years entered the cash economy of Tucson by cutting and selling wood and making baskets. Today they make baskets for the tourist

market, augment Tucson's urban labor force, and operate gambling casinos.

Their harvest of the saguaro cactus fruit, not as regularly as before, is used to make wine for a ceremony to bring rain to the desert.

Papagos still regularly attend services at the San Xavier Mission church on the reservation just outside Tucson. Begun by Father Francisco Eusebio Kino and finished in 1797, the mission is in its bicentennial year. The Papagos were missionized by the Franciscans in the seventeenth century, with the result that they blend folk religion with Catholic ritual and focus on St. Francis.

20

Abe Chanin *interviewed De Grazia for* This Land, These Voices *(1977), coauthored with his wife, Mildred. In Chanin's interview with Jim McNulty in May 1996, he quoted from that early talk with De Grazia.*

"I am going to begin at the age I am," De Grazia told Chanin, "because I am not too interested in the beginning anymore....I'm a part of everybody—part Italian, part Indian, part Mexican, part Jew, part everything. You begin as a seed and then you keep on rolling and rolling like those damned thistles. You roll all over hell...you are just part of all that you've been through, all that has been around you."

22

23

De Grazia *discusses his artistic development, as told by Abe Chanin.*

"There was a time when my colors weren't nice, not brilliant. They were somber. I was painting beggars, people sleeping on the ground, 'borrachos,' and cat houses. One guy in Tucson, Ted Sayles, called that the 'De Grazia God-awful period.' As I got older, my view of life changed and my palette lightened."

San Xavier

Long, long ago a very gentle Jesuit, Padre Kino,
came to northern Mexico and southern Arizona.
He arrived on horseback.
Padre Kino made friends with Indians,
and together they built many churches.
He gave them seeds and showed them
how to grow better crops.
The people loved this good man; they were happy.
The church bells echoed their happiness.
The good padre brought cows and horses.
Padre Kino explored the surrounding land,
establishing ramadas as missions.
By the Santa Cruz River the San Xavier del Bac
Mission was established.
It was to become the most beautiful of his missions.
Years passed and Padre Kino's adobe walls went to dust.
Time was mute.
San Xavier Mission as it stands today was build by the San
Franciscan Padres. But the Church is still known as Padre
Kino's mission.
His spirit is everywhere.

de Grafia 1950

27

Louise DeWald *and her husband, Bud, also a journalist, interviewed Ted from time to time.*

"Ted said things I never have found out for sure were true. He said once he went off on his own (to Mexico) wearing a crucifix and a beard and he was captured by a small tribe who thought he was the reincarnation of Jesus. The chief gave him a daughter for a wife. He was there six weeks.

"I think the thing that shines out in his art is his faith."

a midnight sketch 4 AM

SOME · WALK ✳ · DRINK ✳ PRAY ✳ DANCE ✳ THINK

De Grazia
1964
ARIZONA
USA

30

The Yaquis

Native Name: Yoeme, *1990 Census:* 10,000 in the United States, probably more in Mexico.

The Yaqui historical territory centered in Sonora, Mexico, on the Río Yaqui, stretching south to the Río Cocoraque and north to Guaymas, where it formerly bordered Seri territory.

The Yaqui valley is fertile and the Yaqui people were traditionally farmers. From the time of first contact in the sixteenth century until the twentieth century, the Yaquis were now at peace, now at war with the Spanish and Mexican governments, fighting over the rich farmlands. In the nineteenth century, under the dictatorial Mexican president Porfirio Díaz, government troops began a campaign of exterminating or dispersing the Yaquis. Many fled to what is now southern Arizona, forming several communities of which a half-dozen still exist in the Phoenix and

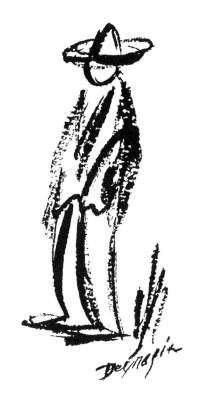

Tucson areas. In Mexico today they occupy the Indigenous Community established for them by President Lázaro Cárdenas in 1939 on roughly one-third of their traditional homelands.

The Yaqui people are probably best known to non-Yaquis for their religion, a blend of Catholicism and Yoeme folk traditions. In Yaqui Arizona villages today, many outsiders attend the Easter Week festival that includes an adaptation of a medieval European passion play. Well known to visitors are the Chapayekas—evil-doers with masks and wooden swords—who want to kill Christ, and the Pascola dancers—wearing wooden masks on the side of the head—who act as ritual hosts and clowns in the festival. Most familiar is the Deer Dancer—wearing a deer's head—whose dancing is believed to bring blessings to the event.

35

Rick Brown, *Sunstone Creations, first met Ted De Grazia in 1970. Sunstone's first commercial product was a De Grazia image laminated onto a wooden plaque. Brown related several anecdotes to Jim Fraser, who interviewed him in March 1996 in Phoenix. Here Brown had driven down to Tucson to get De Grazia's okay for a series of decoupage plaques.*

"Ted and I had gone 'round and 'round about what I wanted to print. He wanted me to do bull-fighters…religious scenes…even a pink mouse eating a watermelon. He wanted me to print that mouse and I said, 'Ted, that's not going to sell for me.' And he said, 'Just watch.'

"So a busload of people were coming in and he went over to meet them. And, of course, the first question that most people ask is, 'What's your favorite painting?' And he said, 'This pink mouse eating a watermelon.' So twenty people bought a print and he came back to me and said, 'See?'"

YAQUI

38

Rick Brown *recalls when De Grazia agreed to have an autograph party at Brown's parents' Hallmark Store in Sun City, Arizona.*

"Ted used to have autograph parties at department stores, and he would always want to have a bottle of whiskey sitting on a table.

"We're not drinkers....I never thought of getting him a bottle of whiskey, and when he came in and didn't see a bottle there, I had to run out to the nearest liquor store and buy one. Old cheapskate me, I bought a small bottle of Old Crow, I think it was. And he polished that thing off and wrote on it, 'This was not big enough.' I still have that bottle at home. It brings back a lot of memories."

40

YAQUI

41

42

The Seris

Native Name: Comaác, *Census:* 500+ (Mexico)

Anthropologists say that Seris have lived along the west coast of Mexico on the Gulf of California since around A.D. 200. They have lived as far to the north as Río Magdalena and south to Río Yaqui, as well as on the gulf islands, San Esteban and Tiburón; today their territory lies between the towns of Bahía Kino and Puerto Libertad.

The Seris have always been fishers, hunters, and gatherers. Historically they were raiders also, but not in modern times. The Seris today have made ironwood carvings of land and marine animals into a tourist industry, which has been pursued on a larger scale by non-Seri Mexican carvers. It is now said to be endangering the "forests" of ironwood—like the mesquite, a variety of acacia.

The Seris have long hunted the sea turtle (now officially endangered) for meat. Regarding it as sacred, they first gutted it, then removed the shell, painted it, and laid it in a special shelter with elephant tree branches covering its head.

Traditional Seri dwellings are shaped like Quonset huts. They are fashioned from parallel branches of bent ocotillo, fastened together with supple twigs, string, and wire and covered with brush, seaweed, and turtle shell—today sometimes also with canvas or plastic.

45

a midnight sketch
LOS SERIS   AGUA July   Deffaai arizona
                              USA 1969

47

De Grazia, *as he was quoted in*
The Irreverent Angel *(1971) by*
Bill Reed:

"How to create! That's something
you can only do by yourself.
Praying may help. Not that I
would pray for help…. I never ask
Christ for favors. He looks tired
to me….

"I don't know what all the fuss is
about. De Grazia ain't so hard to
understand. I'm not so damned
different. Like most people I want
to do something worthwhile with
my life….

"That's my lifeblood hanging
there on the wall. I believe that
being an artist is one of the most
difficult professions in the world.
Nobody believes you're good
until you make it and you begin
to doubt you're good after you
make it. You realize you can never
reach the peak of your own
expectations because there just
isn't enough time."

a midnight sketch of Seri indian

49

Jack Shaeffer, *retired photographer at* The Arizona Daily Star, *knew De Grazia for more than 40 years. He last saw De Grazia in June 1982, three months before the artist's death. A rose society had developed a little tricolor rose and named it in De Grazia's honor, and Shaeffer went to Scottsdale to accept a plant for him.*

"They had a big lunch. I made a little speech and they gave me three roses to bring back—two for Ted and one for me. I took them up to the Gallery in the Sun. Ted was having his good days and his bad days. That was the last time I saw him. I was just a real close friend. Ted, if he liked you, he'd give you the shirt off his back."

a midnight sketch 1a— April   DeGrazia 1976
                                                ARIZONA USA

The Apaches

Native Name: N'de, *1990 Census:* 50,000+

Historically the Apaches included several nomadic
groups who, through raiding and warfare, took over
areas that were homelands of more settled people.
Apaches ranged from southeastern Arizona's San
Pedro Valley, east to northern Texas, south into
northern Chihuahua and Sonora in Mexico, north to
southern Colorado and the area of the Rio Grande
Pueblos, and northwest in Arizona to the Verde Valley
and the Little Colorado. Today, most Apaches live on
several reservations in Arizona and New Mexico.
They are believed by anthropologists to have entered
the American Southwest about the same time as the
Spanish—the late 15th to mid-16th centuries. They
seem to be related, like the Navajo, to the northern
Athapascan people.

As raiders and warriors, the Apaches were often at odds with Spanish, Mexican, and American armies. Geronimo and his people, surrendering to the United States in 1886, were among the latest Apaches to be subdued.

Today the Apaches engage in cattle ranching, the lumber industry, farming, and the operation of ski resorts and gambling casinos as well as other tourist-drawing activities.

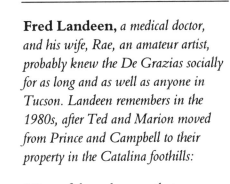

Fred Landeen, *a medical doctor, and his wife, Rae, an amateur artist, probably knew the De Grazias socially for as long and as well as anyone in Tucson. Landeen remembers in the 1980s, after Ted and Marion moved from Prince and Campbell to their property in the Catalina foothills:*

"One of the rules was that every time you came you had to bring five gallons of water, because there was no water and no lights and no gas—there were no amenities there at all."

Fred Landeen *recalls attending a dinner party with the De Grazias:*

"We were having a party and Ross Santee and Olaf Wieghorst were there, and Rae and I and someone else—I can't remember. When we gave a dinner party, I was the cook…and I remember we had hasenpfeffer (rabbit stew), and Ted and Marion got into an argument about hasenpfeffer. Neither of them knew what the hell it was. Ross just sat back and laughed and laughed, and Ted got so mad! He got up and stormed out of the house and said he wouldn't be back. He'd never come back in that house again. He went off someplace. Then, pretty soon, he showed up back at the house as if he'd never left…just came in and sat down and entered into the conversation as though he'd been there every minute of the time."

The Navajos

Native Name: Dineh, *1990 Census:* 200,000+

For the most part the Navajo still live in their historical territory: northwestern New Mexico and northeastern Arizona. Their way of life in the past centered on raiding and farming.

Said to have entered the southwestern United States just before the Spanish, the Navajo are closely related to the Apaches. Their original name was *Apaches de Navaju,* or "Apaches of the Fields" because they have always been farmers and herders. They raided Indian pueblos early on, but in the 1680 Pueblo Revolt, fearing Spanish retaliation, some Pueblo people went to live with the Navajos, who thus became acquainted with Spanish and Pueblo culture. Kit Carson rounded up the Navajo people in 1864 and sent them to the reservation.

In our own time, Navajos tend to earn their livelihood by farming, herding sheep, working silver, weaving rugs, and otherwise serving tourist interests on the Navajo Reservation—particularly at the dramatic and popular tourist site of Monument Valley, part in Arizona, part in Utah, and near the Four Corners where those states are juxtaposed to New Mexico and Colorado.

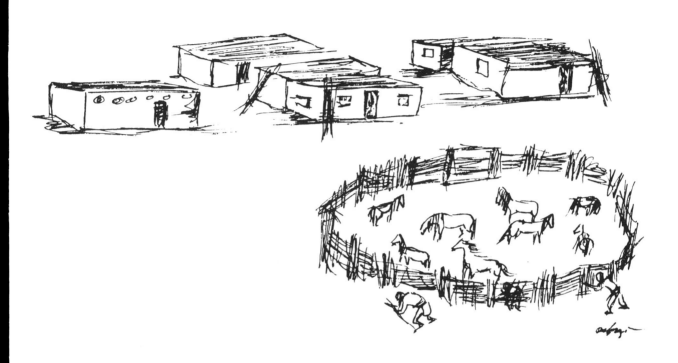

In northern Arizona, a vast land of plains
and nature's sculpted rock monuments
is the land of the Navajo—
their home for a long time
as they range the land
herding their sheep
and living close to the earth.
There is beauty all around,
a sustenance for completeness.

69

Karen Thure *is a freelance writer and editor who with her husband, Terry, worked with De Grazia on some of his publications. She recalls going up to De Grazia's studio:*

"God, those studios were uncomfortable....I mean, little mice running around the place, and dust and cobwebs...not just filthy but definitely debris and the helter-skelter detritus of a brilliant mind that didn't care about all the detail....It was all very impulsive, the way he lived.

"Yeah, he worked real hard, but under what circumstances! When you have that kind of money—I would have gotten an air conditioner ...but he didn't care."

72

73

Credits

ELIZABETH SHAW, longtime De Grazia friend whose memoir introduces this book, has called Tucson home for more than sixty years. After coming here from the midwest to attend college, she was an editor and feature writer for *The Arizona Daily Star*. From 1959 to 1985 she was managing editor of the University of Arizona Press. She presently owns and directs an editorial group in Tucson serving academic publishers across the country.

The publication of this book was made possible through the generous assistance of the DE GRAZIA ART AND CULTURAL FOUNDATION.

Some of the drawings on pages 62–74 first appeared in *They Sang for Horses: The Impact of the Horse on Navajo and Apache Folklore* by LaVerne Harrell Clark (University of Arizona Press, 1966).

Anecdotes contributed by JUNE CALDWELL MARTIN

Ethnographic information furnished by LINDA GREGONIS

Book design and layout by HARRISON SHAFFER

Printing and binding by THOMSON-SHORE INC.

Special thanks to JOSEPH C. WILDER

SAGUESA of the Seri indians   Mexico 1969